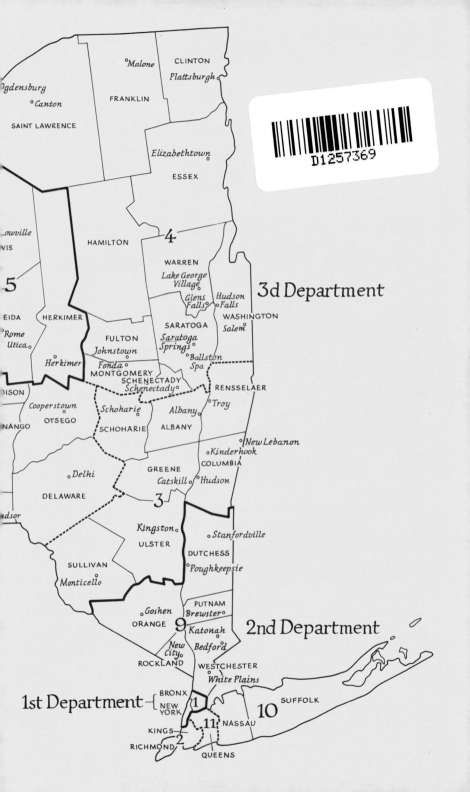

Lawyers and
THE LAW
in New York

Lawyers and
THE LAW
in New York

A Short History And Guide
by Jack Henke

CHARLES EVANS HUGHES PRESS
Albany, New York

Copyright © 1979

CHARLES EVANS HUGHES PRESS

A division of the New York Bar Foundation

One Elk Street, Albany, N.Y. 12207

LIBRARY OF CONGRESS

CATALOGING IN PUBLICATION DATA

Henke, Jack.
Lawyers and the law in New York.

Bibliography: p.
1. Law—New York (State)—History and criticism.
2. Historic sites—New York (State)—Guide-books.
I. Title.
KFN5078.H46   340'.09747   78-10119
ISBN 0-89062-066-0
ISBN 0-89062-065-2 pbk.

ILLUSTRATIONS

Cover: Justice Court in The Back Woods
by Tompkins H. Matteson, 1852, courtesy of
New York State Historical Association, Cooperstown

Milo V. Stewart, pgs. 110, 114, 119, 121, 124, 125,
135, 143, 148, 156, 159, 166

New York Historical Society,
Pirie MacDonald, pg. 64

New York State Office of General Services, pg. 127

Galusha, Catskill Daily Mail, pg. 130

Designed by Michael Lauretano

Produced by the Publishing Center for Cultural Resources,
New York. Manufactured in the United States of America

FOR MY FATHER

Contents

SECTION FIVE

A Guide to Historic Legal Sites in New York

PREFACE

The first trial by jury in the United States ... Zenger v. the Crown, assuring freedom of the press ... three chief justices of the Supreme Court ... six presidents

THE LIST IS ENDLESS, the tradition remarkable, and the men who made it even more so. The story of the growth of New York's bar and bench is one of the brightest chapters in the history of the state. While still a British colony, New York made legal and judicial history and after the bitterness of the Revolution, three extraordinary men, all lawyers, helped bring the stubborn, squabbling colonies together and make them a *United* States: Gouverneur Morris put the Constitution in its final form; John Jay became the first Chief Justice of the United States Supreme Court; and Alexander Hamilton, as the first Secretary of the Treasury, helped to mold and shape the government of the new republic during its crucial first ten years.

The courts of New York State became the model that new states copied when they went about organizing their own judicial institutions and systems. In time, the New York State Bar Association would also be widely copied. Over the years, New York has produced such great and influential jurists as James Kent, Benjamin Cardozo and Learned Hand (jokingly referred to as "the tenth justice of the Supreme Court"), two other Chief Justices, Charles Evans Hughes and Harlan F. Stone. The names roll on: Van Buren, Fillmore, Arthur, Cleveland, Theodore Roosevelt and Franklin D. Roosevelt, New Yorkers and lawyers all. So were George and DeWitt Clinton, William H. Seward, Hamilton Fish, Samuel J. Tilden, Elihu Root, John W. Davis, Alfred E. Smith, Robert F. Wagner, Fiorello LaGuardia, Herbert H. Lehman and Thomas E. Dewey. It is extraordinary that one state has produced so many brilliant and talented men, and that these men all chose to study law.

With such distinguished and imaginative men as governors, legislators and mayors, New York has compiled an unparalleled record of humane and progressive laws, unmatched by any other state.

The first part of this book, Sections One through Four, is a short history of law and lawyers in New York. It traces the gradual appearance and acceptance of men in the legal profession and profiles five distinguished attorneys; describes the development of the judiciary and the judicial system; shows how provincial and state law evolved; gives an account of some landmark New York trials; and summarizes important legislative advances of the nineteenth and early twentieth century.

The book's second and final part is a guide to the Empire State's numerous historic legal sites: the old courthouses, the architecturally rich homes of noted lawyers, judges and governors, and the places where significant legal events took place. These notes will, it is hoped, not only encourage readers to visit the sites described but will add to their enjoyment of them.

At this point I would like to thank several people who have helped with this book. I am particularly indebted to Whitney North Seymour, Jr. and Laurence Vogel of New York City, who coordinated the project and encouraged me at every turn: without their assistance and enthusiasm this book would not have been completed. Hearty thanks are in order, too, to Dr. David Ellis, Professor of History at Hamilton College and a leading if not the leading authority on New York State history; to Joseph Murphy and Thomas Creamer, who edited my original manuscript; to John E. Berry, Executive Director of the New York State Bar Association; to Albert Abrams, former Secretary of the New York State Senate; and finally, to the librarians at Hamilton College and Colgate University, whose patience about the number of overdue books logged out to me ranks with that of Job.

Lawyers in New York

The Birth
of the Legal Profession
in New York State

There was not such a parcel of wild knaves and Jacobites as those that practiced the law in the province of New York, not one of them a barrister, one was a dancing master, another a glover, a third. . .condemned to be hanged in Scotland for blasphemy and burning the bible.—*Governor Bellomont, to the British Treasury Lords, September 8, 1699*

PERRY MASON would have been miserable in colonial New York. He could never have hired Della Street as his secretary nor would he have needed her. If he averaged just one client a year, Mason would have been considered very lucky indeed, for under the colony's first English governors, as under the Dutch directors-general before them, the practice of law was frowned upon, and, although never banned, the hostility toward lawyers made any ambitious man in his right mind look to other fields. As Governor Bellomont's words above suggest, the authorities regarded those who did practice law as unlettered rascals, hardly better than criminals. Gradually, these dubious characters were replaced by more solid men, well versed in the law, who had learned how to make themselves useful to the colony's wealthy merchants and landowners. Official hostility toward them then magically evaporated, and when the sons of New York's great families took up law, the legal profession immediately became acceptable. But the ordinary New Yorker continued to view lawyers with suspicion. It was only after 1765, when a number of colonial lawyers joined the popular protest against Parliament's Stamp Act and other taxes, that plain people at last came to look upon lawyers as useful men—and even as possible protectors and leaders.

11

In New Netherland, with its main settlements of New Amsterdam and Fort Orange (Albany), there were few, if any, trained lawyers. It was the minor court officers, clerks, notaries and secretaries, who would, for a fee, plead on a person's behalf or otherwise help him prepare and present his case. Most often, people who appeared in court, whether as plaintiffs or defendants or as litigants, represented themselves. This was possible because, as in many another frontier community, the judge was often as unacquainted with the law as the common man standing before him, hat in hand. Decisions were made on a practical basis, with little leafing through the statutes—that is, if the judge could read in the first place.

Most actions, both civil and criminal, were brought before the Dutch colonial court, consisting of six men: the director-general and the four members of his council, all appointed by the directors of the Dutch West India Company in far-off Amsterdam, plus an officer, called the *schout*, appointed by the director-general himself. The real concern of all six magistrates was to look after the interests of their common employer, the Dutch West India Company. The *schout* was also the colony's district attorney and sheriff and functioned in court as the prosecutor, and, astonishingly, sometimes as the defense attorney as well—presumably losing when he won and winning when he lost. The *schout* was expected to ferret out the facts through questioning witnesses. Although one of his duties was to explain the law to the citizenry, most *schouts*, chosen for their loyalty to the director-general rather than their learning, were not better informed in Dutch-Roman law than the average layman. Paradoxically, the average layman in colonial New York probably knew more law, and certainly knew more about court procedure, than the New Yorker of today, for in New Netherland, where little public entertainment was available, sessions of the court were well attended, simply for the lack of something better to do.

Some men dealing with the courts were occasionally begrudged the dignity of the title "attorney," and appeared to know a little law. Their obvious scorn for the judges is illustrated by the reaction of one reckless fellow, Waldewyn van der Veen,

who became so exasperated when he lost a case that he spoke of
the magistrates as "simpletons and blockheads." Simpletons and
blockheads they may well have been but they had the power to
find van der Veen in contempt and they sentenced him to "beg
forgiveness, with uncovered head, to God, Justice and the Wor-
shipful Court, and moreover to pay as a fine 190 guilders." Late
in the Dutch occupation, when many English had settled in New
Netherland, notaries who were fluent in Dutch and English
earned handsome fees, but more for their linguistic abilities
than for their legal abilities.

What little work did come the lawyer's way soon disappeared
when the Dutch colonial government introduced arbitrators to
help judges reach a verdict. The *coup de grâce* was the fixing of
attorneys' fees by the Dutch West India Company and its decision that lawyers could not charge the poor a fee.

In 1664, the British seized New Netherland, and renamed the
entire colony and its main settlement New York. The new governor overhauled legal and judicial institutions and procedures,
and introduced, for the first time in the New World, guarantees
of a trial by jury. A giant step. But even so, the climate for the
practice of law was, if anything, even more unfavorable than
before. New York was not a royal colony but the personal property of King Charles's younger brother James, Duke of York.
The king's patent granting the colony to him did not require the
duke to proclaim English Common Law as the rule of the land
but simply to refrain from making laws that conflicted with those
of England. In effect, the laws he decreed, known as the Duke's
Laws, left things pretty much as they had been under the Dutch.
Arbitration continued to play a major part in arriving at a verdict. Judges exercised far more authority than they could have if
Common Law had been observed. They decided cases on the
basis of general, theoretical rules of justice rather than according to law and precedent. And when the Duke's council decreed
that citizens' legal needs could be taken care of by a public magistrate, the lawyer all but vanished from the scene. When it came
to representing clients in court, knowledge of Common Law
meant little and might even, indeed, have counted against a

magistrate rash enough to parade such knowledge.

Suspicion of the lawyers ran deep. It was feared that unless lawyers were kept firmly in check, they would stir up harmful litigation, destroying peace and order, so the Duke's Laws went even further and provided that anyone "indicted and proved and Judged a common Barrator" could be fined and imprisoned.

On the death of King Charles in 1685, New York's distant landlord, the duke, succeeded him as James II. In only three years, James was dethroned because of his Catholicism, and Parliament replaced him with his daughter Mary and her Dutch husband, William, Prince of Orange, both good Protestants and firmly against "Popery." In New York, confusion reigned until, in 1691, William and Mary's choice as governor, Colonel Henry Sloughter, arrived to restore order. Sloughter convened an assembly, which set into motion sweeping judicial reforms. Most importantly, it established Common Law as the fundamental law of the province. From then on, cases were decided, as in England, by referring to that voluminous body of ancient and modern laws, and to judicial precedent. All at once, a knowledge of the law was necessary to keep the legal machinery functioning, and lawyers, no longer looked upon as dangerous meddlers, became officers of the courts, and played a key role in trials, hearings and all legal matters.

In response to this heady elevation of their status, and to the increased demand for their services, the number of lawyers practicing in New York doubled between 1691 and 1712. At the same time, their caliber improved appreciably. Many of the new lawyers had served as clerks in British courts, and a few were even graduates of the famous Inns of Court in London. In 1709, a group of enterprising lawyers met to form a bar association, so that attorneys' fees could be regulated. In 1728, a grievance committee was formed to combat unfair legal practices. The bar association and grievance committee were the first to be organized in the thirteen colonies.

Since their work involved them continually with the colonial authorities who conducted New York's affairs for King and Parliament, lawyers had to keep a finger on the political pulse. Although many of them held very conservative views, because of their business and family ties to the aristocracy, they did not hesitate to guard against what they considered excessive claims or abuses on the part of the colonial authorities, King or Parliament. Several well-known lawyers, for example, came to the defense of the printer John Peter Zenger, who attacked the autocratic and unpopular Governor William Cosby in his newspaper, causing the governor to charge him with libel. Zenger was defended by the colonies' most illustrious lawyers and his acquittal in 1735 was acclaimed as a victory for freedom of the press. This landmark decision was the basis for the guarantees found in the Constitution, which protect our free press to this day.

As the lawyers' influence in the community grew, their opinions carried greater weight. Yet something of their former scandalous reputation still clung to them. That, plus their obvious connections with the colony's establishment, hardly endeared them to the less privileged. The wealthy landowner, lawyer and future judge, Robert Livingston, wrote in 1745 that "There is perhaps no set of men that bear so ill a character in the estimation of the vulgar, as the gentlemen of the long robe."

Since there were no law schools in the colony of New York, young men hoping one day to don the long robe learned their profession by apprenticing themselves to lawyers. After at least two years of college, an aspiring lawyer had to put in another two years or more as a clerk in an attorney's office. During apprenticeship, he had to absorb a curriculum that included "the English, Latin and French tongues, writing, arithmetick, geometry, surveying, merchants' accounts or bookkeeping, geography, chronology, history, logick and rhetoric, Divinity, the law of nature and nations, and the law of England." Once the young man had given proof of his grasp of these extraordinarily varied subjects he could practice law, but he was still bound to his master and mentor for another five years.

The standard fees charged by colonial New York lawyers give a clue to their methods and priorities. For examining a witness,

CARTER, LEDYARD & MILBURN
COUNSELLORS AT LAW
54 WALL STREET
NEW YORK

LEWIS CASS LEDYARD
JOHN G. MILBURN
EDMUND L. BAYLIES
GEORGE A. MILLER
LEWIS CASS LEDYARD, JR.
WALTER F. TAYLOR
JOSEPH W. WELSH

June 10th, 1907.

Mr. F. Roosevelt,
    135 East 36th Street,
        New York City.

Dear Mr. Roosevelt:-

    I have talked over with Mr. Ledyard the question of your coming to our office, and I find that we can arrange to have a place for you at such time as you may wish to come here in the autumn, not later than October 1st, preferably a week or so earlier.

    In case you come to us the arrangement with you will be the same as we usually make in such cases, that is to say, you will come to us the first year without salary, and after you have been with us for a year we would expect, if you remain, to pay you a salary which, however, at the outset would necessarily be rather small.

                    Very truly yours,

                    Edmund L. Baylies

---

*Young Franklin Roosevelt was apprenticed,
just as his colonial predecessors were.*

an attorney received four shillings. "Arguing in opposition to any motion with success" cost a client five shillings, as did "every motion that would be proper in Westminster Hall." The "fee on trial or inquest, or in error" was twelve shillings. And "traveling charges on the circuits [circuit courts] for each day" came to thirteen shillings fourpence.

By the middle of the eighteenth century New York's lawyers were firmly established in the colony's economic life. They enjoyed the confidence of the "aristocracy" of landowners and merchants who controlled New York. They cordially welcomed their lawyer friends into the upper ranks of colonial society. And in the ten or twelve years following the end of the French and Indian War, these colonial lawyers became independent enough to overcome the suspicion that they were simply lackeys of the rich, and, as such, uncritical upholders of the status quo. When

16

Lieutenant Governor Cadwallader Colden sought to take over the supreme court's function of hearing appeals from the lower courts, he could not find a single lawyer in the colony willing to argue his case. When Parliament levied special taxes on the colonies, lawyers took the lead in refusing to pay them. Not only did they speak out against them, some, notably John Lamb and Alexander McDougall, helped found a patriotic colonial organization called the Sons of Liberty. And when sentiment grew for concerted action by the colonies, many New York lawyers sat on grievance committees and attended meetings of the Continental Congress. By the eve of the American Revolution, it was clear that New York lawyers had done much to bring about the impending confrontation with the Crown, in spite of the fact that most of them still did not wish total independence from Britain and shrank from the thought of taking up arms against the King.

In three quarters of a century the lawyers of New York had come a long way. No longer could they be called "a parcel of wild knaves and Jacobites." Rather, they were proud members of a leading profession, admired, by and large, for their learning, their devotion to democratic ideals, their belief in justice, and, most of all, for their high ethical standards.

Frontier Justice:
Lawyers on Horseback

A pioneer society does not believe in specialists nor in an organized profession of lawyers. The pioneer feels himself equal to anything and prefers to believe that he can prosecute, defend and judge his own law suits.—Roscoe Pound, in an address to the Brooklyn Law School, 1928

ALTHOUGH NEW AMSTERDAM was an outpost of European civilization on the frontier of a vast, unknown wilderness, it was not entirely a pioneer community. With its company-appointed officials, its courts and churches, and its military garrison, it was more like a transplanted piece of maritime Holland. As it grew more populous and secure, under the Dutch and then the British, its frontier character became even less apparent. Contrary to Dean Pound's remarks, the people of New Amsterdam and New York did not feel as antagonistic toward lawyers as the colonial officials did. It was the magistrates, in particular, who feared that lawyers might undercut their authority and challenge the control of the Dutch West India Company. When the British won New York, lawyers were still thought to be dangerous and likely to defy edicts from the Duke of York.

Pioneer settlements did exist in remote sections of New Netherland and New York colony. However, it was independence from British rule that touched off an explosion of pioneering. Now we see Dean Pound's theories at work. Clearing the land of trees, plowing and planting their fields, and attending to all their own needs, physical and spiritual, while keeping a careful eye on the ever-present Indian, pioneer families learned to rely on themselves and their neighbors for everything. And the more they did, the less willing were they to put up with the restrictions that townsmen had accepted as the price of security. They found the law, with its pettifogging insistence on precedents set long ago, in a remote and settled England, utterly unlike their own wild surroundings, ludicrously inapplicable. As later frontiersmen were to do every step westward in the coming century, they simply ignored what the law books said, turning instead to simple, rough-and-ready courtroom procedures, based on what the majority of people felt was right. In other words: frontier justice.

After the Revolution, much of New York State was a kind of battleground between town and frontier, where the courts, backed by the power of the state, came up against the stubborn resistance of people who understood only frontier justice. People who were impatient with, and suspicious of, town law. The clash between these totally separate and wary groups is vividly illustrated by an account written in 1787 by Dirck Gardenier, describing his attempt to serve an eviction notice on an upstate farmer:

18

I found a Number of People at work for him [the farmer] in Harvest. I gave his wife the Ejectt. & Read the letter of Mr. Stout. I Tould her besides the Contents & then made to the Door. She Desired Id stay untill her Husband came home who was in sight. I went on my Horse & then stopt. When he came up he asked me what I left that paper for. I tould him I had no further use for it. He foamed at the mouth his Limbs shook his Voise faltered. Seized hold of my Bridle & Tould me to take back the paper or he would send me into Eternaty in a Moment with Many Bitter oaths to inforce a belief. I was obliged to take back the paper as I saw a number Making up towards the hous. When I had the paper he let me lose the Rains. I Trowed Down the paper & put speed to my Departure. He called for his horse & some. My horse not being of the best we Measured the ground as fast as we could and at Majr Duglas's they overtook me to the number of about fifteen. However I got in the House before them & fastned the Door. They Demanded admittence which Majr Duglas Refused. They Brandished their Clubs swore they would have me Dead or alive or I must go & Take the Ejectt back.

Gardenier, obviously not suicidal, took back the "Ejectt," but the farmer was the final loser against the power of the courts, and was eventually evicted.

In frontier country, the local judge personified the law, and, on occasion, had to prove his own worth off the bench as well as on it. Judge Hugh White, the first settler of Whitestown, once unexpectedly found the burden of proof thrust upon him at an impromptu wrestling match arranged by Oneida braves. The following account of the event shows Judge White to be a wily manipulator:

After a number of trials had been made, in which the chief came off the conqueror, he came forward and challenged the settler [Judge White] to a clinch with him. This was done in a manner, and with a degree of braggadocio, that convinced the Judge that if he refused the encounter it would subject him to the constant inconveniences of being brow-beaten by the Indian, and cost him the trouble of being believed a coward. . . . He therefore accepted the challenge and took hold with the Indian, and by a fortunate trip, succeeded almost instantly in throwing him. As he saw him falling, in order to prevent the necessity of ever making another trial of his powers, and of receiving any new challenge, he contrived to fall with all his weight, he then constituting an avoirdupois of some 250 lbs., upon the Indian. The weight for an instant drove all the breath from the poor fellow's body; and it was some moments before he could get up. At length he slowly arose, shrugged his shoulders with an emphatic "Ugh! you good fellow too much!" I need not add that he was never afterwards challenged to wrestle with an Indian.

In that long-vanished time, quick thinking was less a virtue than a necessity for survival in the thinly settled countryside of upstate New York. And as the record below shows, lawyers and judges were as quick as other citizens at finding solutions to the problem that found them.

At the first term of a court, held in January, 1794, within the limits of Oneida County as now constituted, Sheriff Colbreth was in attendance and the weather was intensely cold. The church building in New Hartford, in which the court was convened, was unheated and as night drew near, the members of the bar found the condition unendurable, so they induced the sheriff to repair to a neighboring inn and procure a jug of spirits.

Upon the jug's appearing, it was passed around the bar table and each of the learned counsellors in his turn upraised the elegant vessel and by the simplest process imaginable, partook of so much as he deemed a sufficient dose of the delicious fluid.

While this operation was proceeding, the three judges held a consultation and the first judge announced that he saw no reason why they should sit there and freeze to death and ordered the crier to adjourn the court, whereupon Sheriff Colbreth hastily passed the jug to the bench saying, "No, no, no, judge, don't adjourn; take a little gin, judge, that will keep you warm."

The court did not adjourn that freezing January day. Besides brawn, energy and stamina, what counted for most in the hinterland were native intelligence and common sense. Apart from a scattering of ministers and schoolmasters, there were few people of education in the region. This was also true of lawyers. After the Revolution, a lingering dislike of Britain and things British discouraged the study of Common Law. Some hot-headed judges even refused to allow lawyers to cite it in court. Sadly, the body of new federal and state law was meager—so meager, in fact, that in three months a diligent young man could learn everything he needed to know to practice law. Lawyers became discouraged about learning any technicalities since the pioneers had boundless confidence in their own ability to resolve all problems, including the knottiest legal ones. They preferred to make their own decisions rather than study centuries of legal interpretations and niceties. More than one frontier judge dismissed the works of Coke and Blackstone, revered almost as holy writ in New York City courts, as mere irrelevancies.

Consequently, men with little education and even less knowledge of the law were often appointed to the bench in country districts. They were chosen on the basis of their character, their standing in the community and their proven patriotism. One such worthy was Colonel Heinrich Staring, a Revolutionary War hero who became the first member of the Court of Common Pleas of Herkimer County. His Honor was able to write his name well enough but he could not read, a disability that was to occasion him some inconvenience.

A New York law of those days prohibited "all unnecessary labor and travelling on the first day of the week, commonly called Sunday." One Sunday, Staring arrested a man riding east to his home in Massachusetts and fined him the customary six "York shillings." Paying up, the Yankee asked the judge to issue him a pass that would protect him from further arrest and fines on his long trip home. Staring, not wishing to confess his illiteracy, ordered the Yankee to draw up the pass, which he signed with a flourish. The stranger thanked him, pocketed the paper and quickly rode off. Staring thought no more about the matter until, months later, he went into a store in Canajoharie, and was accosted by the proprietor, who produced a handwritten draft for twenty-five dollars and asked him to pay on the spot. An account of the incident reads:

At first he strenuously denied having given such an order, but having more particularly examined the signature, and finding it genuine, he revolved the matter over in his mind, and at last caught an inkling of the puss at the bottom of the meal-tub. He asked for a description of the person who presented the order, when the Yankee and his beast were most accurately described. "Oh! Now I know it all," says the Judge, "it is nothing but that Yankees pass." As the signature was genuine, and as no proof could be made of the fraud, the draft had to be duly honored.

But the frontier was disappearing: even as Judge Staring paid the scoundrel Yankee's bill, as Judge White downed his Indian and as the Oneida judges gulped their gin. The farmlands were being invaded by commerce and industry, particularly in the form of textile mills. As the frontier moved west, so, inevitably, did the informal, raucous brand of justice that these men represented. The pace of change accelerated. In 1807 Robert Fulton proved, on the Hudson, that steam power could move ships, and the War of 1812 brought a boom in shipbuilding to Lake Champlain and Lake Erie. In 1825 the opening of the Erie Canal linked the Atlantic to the Great Lakes, spurring the growth and prosperity not only of the canal's saltwater terminal, New York City, but of the cities it passed through: Schenectady, Utica, Rome, Syracuse, Buffalo. After 1831 railroads began to crisscross the state, and for the rest of the nineteenth century New York remained the country's most important artery for commercial traffic between East and West.

During this time of rapid change, new law upon new law was passed, especially in the area of commerce, transportation and manufacturing. To cope with the vastly increased and much more complex demands of the new industrial society, standards for selecting judges and lawyers became higher and the gulf separating upstate from downstate narrowed as far as the practice of law was concerned.

Meanwhile, after about 1820, a band of able and ambitious upstate lawyers, led by future President Martin Van Buren, introduced something quite new to America: a disciplined political machine. The Albany Regency, as it was called, controlled the Democratic Party in New York, the country's most populous state, and also wielded enormous national influence. Its members held many high offices, until, in 1842, the Regency split over the question of the extension of slavery in the new western territories. A number of New York lawyers were uncompromising foes of slavery, most notably William H. Seward, a former Governor, Senator, presidential candidate and Secretary of State throughout the Civil War.

By the time of the Civil War, frontier justice was a long-vanished memory even in the remotest corners of the state. But a hint of its irreverent rustic humor survived in an anecdote, published in 1867, about a courtroom exchange that took place in Secretary Seward's home town.

On a trial at Auburn, the counsel for the people, after severely cross-examining a witness, suddenly put on a look of severity and said: "Mr. Witness, has not an effort been made to induce you to tell a different story?"

"A different story from what I have told you, sir?"

"That is what I mean."

"Yes, sir; several persons have tried to get me to tell a different story from what I have told, but they couldn't."

"Now, sir! upon your oath, I wish to know who those persons are!"

"Waal, I guess you've tried 'bout as hard as any of 'em."

Closing Ranks:
The Bar Organizes

To maintain the honor and dignity of the profession of the law, to increase its usefulness in promoting the due administration of justice, and to cultivate social intercourse among its members.— Objectives of the New York City Bar Association, 1870

IN RESPONSE to the demand for war matériel during the Civil War, American industry, almost all of it in the North, had greatly expanded. When peace came, the factories and mills turned to supplying the needs of a large and fast-growing population swollen by immigration. For men with money to spare, there were many opportunities to get rich quick. And their goal could be speedily attained, nay, guaranteed, with the connivance of legislators ready to pass laws facilitating such schemes and judges willing to make decisions that favored them.

Corruption flourished, and in New York, the nation's financial capital, the monies made by illegal or extra-legal means were staggering. As the collaboration between unprincipled entrepreneurs and corrupt lawyers and judges became more conspicuous, the legal profession was once more in disgrace.

At the time, the city was in the clutches of the Tweed Ring, a corrupt and powerful group headed by William Marcy Tweed, which dominated Tammany Hall. Tweed, who had performed "useful" services for the robber baron railroad builders Jay Gould and Jim Fisk, was now systematically plundering the city treasury, protected by judges he had appointed. In 1869 *The New York Times,* voicing the indignation of the city's more conscientious citizens, urged New York's lawyers to lend a hand in cleaning up the mess:

If it be the supineness, the guilty silence of the lawyers, as officers of the people's courts, which have brought us to our present pass, it is their reawakened public spirit and activity which must help us back to a better state of things. . . . We must again proclaim that the bar must lead the way.

Stung by this Olympian criticism as well as the less temperate taunts of other newspapers, many lawyers leaped to respond to the *Times'* appeal. Their logical first step, as they saw it, was to set their own house in order. A committee of lawyers under the chairmanship of William M. Evarts drew up a letter calling on the city's lawyers to organize themselves into a bar association, as their colonial predecessors had done 160 years before. Part of Evarts' letter read:

It seems like an abdication of its legitimate position that the Bar of the City of New York, numbering its members by thousands, should have absolutely no organization whatever; that its influence in all matters affecting either its own dignity and interests as a profession, or the general good as connected with the advancement of jurisprudence or reforms in the adminstration of justice, should be only that divided and dispersed influence of its

Samuel J. Tilden, whose brilliant accomplishments include being one of the founders of the Association of the Bar of the City of New York.

members, which from being divided and dispersed, goes for nothing.

At a meeting held on February 1, 1870, the New York City Bar Association was duly organized. Most of the members spoke of the need to correct judicial abuses and raise professional standards. The objectives of the new organization were most eloquently stated by Samuel J. Tilden, a reform-minded political leader who was soon to gain national fame for smashing the Tweed Ring. History would also record him as the man who received more popular votes than his opponent, Rutherford B. Hayes, in the Presidential election of 1876, but who lost in the Electoral College, where the Republicans had a one-vote majority.

Tilden announced to the newly organized city bar association:

The bar, if it is to continue to exist, if it would restore itself to the dignity and honor which it once possessed, must be bold in defense, and, if need be, bold in aggression. If it will do its duty to itself, if it will do its duty to the profession which it follows and to which it is devoted, the bar can do everything else. It can have reformed constitutions, it can have a reformed judiciary, it can have the administration of justice made pure and honorable, and can restore both the judiciary and the bar until it shall be once more, as it formerly was, an honorable and an elevated calling.

The association's various committees soon got down to business. A year later, the group investigating judicial abuses issued a damaging, thoroughly documented report on the conduct of certain city judges. The report, well publicized, brought quick action. One Tweed appointee resigned from the bench, another was removed by unanimous vote of the state senate, and a third was impeached, tried and found guilty by the Court of Appeals.

Meanwhile, other committees sought to improve standards within the profession. A grievance committee began to look routinely into complaints of misconduct by lawyers, while another set out to frame a professional code of ethics. As a result of yet another committee report, the association demanded stricter requirements for admission to the bar, calling for tougher examinations and tighter licensing.

Early in 1876, the association petitioned the state government to require attendance at law school for two years, a year of work as a law clerk, plus passing the bar examinations before permission to practice law was granted. In April, the Court of Appeals approved the suggested requirements.

At the same time that the new requirements were being considered, it was suggested that a state bar association be formed. Elliott F. Shepard, a noted lawyer, set in motion the committees, subcommittees, boards and appointees that, after laboring for a full year, brought together ninety-one delegates in the Old Capitol building in Albany to set up the state bar association. At "3½ o'clock P.M.," November 21, 1876, the delegates formally declared the existence of the New York State Bar Association and went to work writing its constitution and by-laws. The following spring, by an act of the legislature, the New York State Bar Association was incorporated, with John K. Porter as president and with Charles W. Sanford, Samuel Hand, John J. Armstrong, William Ruger, Horatio Ballard, James Angle and Myron H. Peck as vice-presidents, each representing a judicial district.

Seventy-five years later Nathan L. Miller, a former president
of the association and former governor of New York, summa-
rized the history of the association in an article in the *New York
State Bar Bulletin* for December, 1952. Here are some of the
highlights Governor Miller cited:

In 1896, as a result perhaps of the tension between this country
and England, the Association held a special meeting, approved
and adopted a plan for an International Court to settle international disputes and a memorial to the Congress and the President urging the adoption of the plan. Thus to the New York
State Bar Association belongs the credit of having on its own
initiative formulated and promoted the adoption of a plan on
international arbitration which resulted in the present World
Court.

In 1904, the Association took the initiative in an effort which
resulted in our Consolidated Laws.

In 1910, after many years of effort, the Association finally
succeeded in procuring legislation effecting many needed reforms in Surrogate's procedure and appellate practice.

In 1912 the Association took the initiative in securing the
removal of the Court of Appeals from its inadequate quarters in
the Capitol to the Old State Hall, an historic building which now
stands as a monument to the Association's efficiency and public
spirit.

Again, it initiated the effort which led to the creation in 1934
of the Judicial Council, which has become an important and
influential body in the work of law reform.

There can be no more important or useful work than the
extension of legal aid to those in need of it, who have not the
ability to pay. The Association's work in that field has been
greatly intensified in recent years. This is a work which all of the
Associations, State, City and County, must share. Much has been
accomplished. More and more people, however humble, may
now receive needed legal advice and service within their means.

The Association has played a leading role in securing the
adoption of uniform State laws. Indeed, it initiated the effort.
Much has been accomplished. More remains to be done.

And in fact more *was* done. When, for example, President
Franklin D. Roosevelt, in 1937, sought to "pack" the Supreme
Court by appointing six more associate justices in addition to the

existing nine, the New York State Bar Association actively opposed the move. Roosevelt's maneuver was, in the end, over-
whelmingly defeated by Congress. Chief Justice Charles Evans
Hughes, a one-time president of the New York State Bar Association, worked hard behind the scenes, when tempers were
anything but cool, to keep a degree of calm, if not dignity, between the contending parties. In 1941, the Association lobbied
hard for New York's Motor Vehicle Safety Act. And in 1947 it
played host to the first international conference on the legal
profession ever held.

In 1968 the Association was instrumental in arranging New
York's unprecedented Fair Trial-Free Press Conference, whose
purpose was "to give shape to an ongoing dialogue between the
news media and the law enforcement agencies." Five years later,
it instituted the practice of forming and fielding "action units,"
which are actually task forces designed to perform their duties
on a crash basis, and to react with equal speed, if need be, in a
crisis. Three units have already achieved important gains: one in
judicial reform, a second in legislative reforms , and a third unit
on procedures to improve the availability of legal services.

For close to three centuries now, from the days of the colonial
barrister through those of the frontier judge and down to our
own time, the organized profession of the law in New York has
provided a service vital to the affairs of the colony and state. Its
members have not always enjoyed, nor have they always de-
served, the public's admiration, yet at most times they have stood
high in the esteem of their fellow citizens. And with good reason. For they have contributed, out of all proportion to their
numbers, to leadership and well-being of their communities.

Throughout the hundred years of its existence, the New York
State Bar Association has quietly but consistently worked to ad-
vance the worthiest ideals of the legal profession. How well it has
succeeded is perhaps best summed up, not in elaborate prose,
but in a sentence written by its former president, Nathan Miller.
"With such a history," he wrote, "and such an organization, its
continued usefulness is assured."

Such an organization indeed!

The Law in New York

The Dutch &
Early English Colonial Periods
1609-91

IN THE YEAR 1609 two European explorers, totally unaware of each other, set out from points hundreds of miles apart, to investigate the vast wilderness that would one day be the colony of New York. From Canada, Samuel de Champlain voyaged south down the long lake that now bears his name. Soon other Frenchmen, trappers and Jesuit missionaries, followed him and penetrated the northern and western reaches of that territory. South, from the ocean harbor at the mouth of the river later to be named for him, Henry Hudson, an Englishman in the employ of the Dutch East India Company, sailed upriver, almost to the site of present-day Albany.

Four years later, Dutch merchants set up a trading post near that spot. Furs and beaver skins were shipped down the river and then sent by sea to distant Holland. In 1621 a group of businessmen met in Amsterdam and founded the Dutch West India Company. They hoped to reap huge profits in the South Atlantic from the West African trade and dreamed of capturing rich Brazil from the Portuguese. But North America, too, had a place in their plans. In 1624 they dispatched thirty families, Dutch- and French-speaking Walloons, to the commodious harbor Henry Hudson had claimed for them. Some continued up the river to build Fort Orange near the Albany trading post, the others settled on Little Nut (now Governors) Island. The following year, the families on Nut Island were ferried over to the tip of the big island of Manhattan, where the men set to work building a fort. And in 1626 Peter Minuit, sent over by the company as director general of the colony, purchased Manhattan from the local Indians for the celebrated twenty-four dollars, or sixty guilders.

Minuit would have to temporarily recall the Fort Orange settlers when the Indians of the surrounding countryside went on
the warpath, but New Netherland and its principal settlement
and capital, New Amsterdam, were now firmly established.

A Frontier Society

SHIPS HAD BROUGHT the colonists to New Netherland and
would bring others, together with livestock, tools and supplies.
Ships constituted their vital link with their homeland; and ships,
naturally enough, provided them with a model for their society,
which was organized more or less in line with the rules and
customs regulating life on board a Dutch merchantship. Like a
ship's captain and his officers, the director general and his council held sole and total command. All were handpicked by the
company's directors in Amsterdam, and from time to time, they
would include the captain of whatever Dutch West India ship
that happened to be in port. As for the ordinary colonists, few
were free agents, the majority being bound to the company by
contract. In theory, they enjoyed no more rights than ordinary
seamen. Actually, they were often unruly and showed little respect for authority, taking pleasure in puncturing the pompous-
ness of any strutting dignitary.

Present-day New Yorkers who lament that their vast metrop-
olis has become ungovernable might be startled to learn that
several Dutch directors general found New Amsterdam very
nearly impossible to govern at a time when its population was no
more than a few hundred souls. Those early citizens were vigi-
lant in defending their individual liberties, and reluctant, like all
frontier people, to take orders.

Dispensing Justice
in Town & Country

THE LAWS by which New Netherland was governed were, of
course, those of the mother country, in particular the customs

30

and ordinances then in effect in the provinces of Holland and Zeeland. These could be amended, however, by the directors' instructions or the terms of the contracts they made with persons, families and groups coming to New Netherland. The director general and his council were granted the power to make their own laws, subject to ratification in Amsterdam. They were, consequently, both the colony's executive and legislative branches. And they were, finally, its judiciary as well, since the director general and his council were also the magistrates.

The key officer of this court was the formidable *schout*, that legal jack-of-all-trades whose decisions could only be changed by the director general or appealed in Amsterdam to the Dutch States-General, and then only if the case involved capital punishment. In addition, the *schout* transmitted court proceedings to the Dutch West India Company and published and executed all laws, including customs regulations.

Because the Dutch in the Netherlands enjoyed religious liberty and a relatively high standard of living, they had less incentive than most Europeans to emigrate, with the result that New Netherland soon suffered from lack of settlers. To encourage settlers, the West India Company issued a Charter of Freedoms and Exemptions providing that "private persons" could take all the land they were able to farm. Another provision promised immense tracts of land to anyone who would recruit, equip and send fifty settlers over. These "private persons" and recruiters, often monied lesser sons of aristocrats, were called *patroons* and not under the control of the Company. They were law unto themselves. Several wealthy men accepted the challenge and became patroons, living in Amsterdam for the most part and directing their estates from afar. Within a few years most of their plantations failed, only Kiliaen van Rensselaer, a prosperous diamond merchant in Amsterdam, succeeded in keeping his huge holding, Rensselaerswyck. The domain consisted of most of the present counties of Albany, Rensselaer and much of Columbia. In 1634, through his agent at Rensselaerswyck, van Rensselaer appointed a *schout* to preside over a patroon's court, the first local court in the colony. It was entirely composed of plain farmers, who presumably judged each case with little or no reference to laws or codes, since they knew next to nothing about them, and simply decided each case on its merits, as they saw it.

Confusion Reigns

MEANWHILE, PETER MINUIT had been recalled to Holland and a nephew of van Rensselaer, Wouter van Twiller, was sent over in his place. The new director general irritated and alienated his countrymen with his blundering ways, and in 1637 he left "a colony fraught with confusion." Promptly, on arriving the following year, the next director general, William Kieft, seized absolute control. If van Twiller's ineptitude had made him the butt of ridicule, Kieft's arbitrary rule was still less to the colonists' liking. Worse, his tactlessness toward the Indians turned them against the colonists, who had always been friendly to the neighboring tribes. Now they were forced to defend the town from attack, resulting in many casualties.

In the summer of 1641 and again in the fall of 1643, military emergencies caused by trouble with the Indians forced Kieft to accept a panel of advisers, chosen by the leading families. Each time, the advisers petitioned for reforms and less control in the hands of Kieft. On the second occasion, the advisers appealed over his head directly to the company in highly critical terms. At last, in 1647, Kieft was recalled to Holland to answer the colonists' charges, only to be lost at sea on the way. The colony's last and greatest director general had already arrived, a crusty company official sporting a wooden leg, replacing the one smashed by a cannonball in the West Indies: the redoubtable Peter Stuyvesant.

Loose Talk & the Law

WHILE THE PEOPLE of New Amsterdam respected property— instances of theft appear to have been comparatively rare—their respect did not extend to reputations, to judge by the number of actions for slander and libel that were brought before the magistrates. Between April 1638 and April 1639, for example, the provincial court heard fifty civil and forty-three criminal cases. Of the latter, no few than twenty-eight were suits alleging defamation of character. But if such figures suggest that New Amsterdamers were fond of insulting one another but not all that fond of being the victim of name-calling, they were extremely sensitive to the finer points of personal honor. Very commonly a man or woman would be dragged into court accused of nothing more heinous than, in the heat of anger, having called someone a mildly unflattering name like "black pudding" or "Dutch dough-face," "swine" or "*verlickker*" (tale-bearer). When it came to the bandying about of such terrible epithets as "horned beast" (cuckold) and "*moff*" (the term applied in Holland to the despised Germans) one can see that the injured party had little choice but to go to law.

Their High Mightinesses, as the magistrates were styled, were also very touchy about their dignity. A particular thorn in their side was notaries with some knowledge of the law, which usually meant it exceeded their own. If someone was bold enough to quote from Dutch-Roman law, their vengeance was often swift and severe. The magistrates *were* the law and no one was allowed to forget it.

Several cases between 1638 and 1639 illuminate the Dutch court of the day, and they all concerned Anthony Jansen, a curious man, to say the least, who managed to involve himself in fifteen different law suits that year.

Jansen was a colorful character, who needed only to speak to bring forth an explosive reaction. A mulatto sometimes referred to as "Anthony the Turk", Jansen and his wife, Grietse Reyniers, ran a small farm. They were argumentative people, possibly because it was whispered, and not too softly, that Grietse was a "loose woman." At one trial, a midwife testified that Grietse had asked her whom her new baby resembled: her husband or Andries Hudden, once a Council member. One man, at another inquiry, testified that Grietse, in reply to the yells from a ship's crew along the East River docks, "lifted up her petticoat and [turning to] the crew pointed to her behind."

In each of Jansen's cases, decisions were, of course, made by the Director and Council, serving as magistrates, and the *schout*. In the Dutch court procedures, after the testimony of the Jansens and the various plaintiffs was recorded, witnesses were summoned. These were primarily character or, in this case, "anti-character" witnesses. Much of the evidence was hearsay and, while it would not carry any weight in courts today, it counted for a great deal in the Dutch judicial system. In most cases the Jansens were required to pay trial costs, but even this failed to cool down their hot-blooded taunts and lawlessness.

The issues involved in the Jansens' cases resembled most of the suits tried in New Netherland's courts. The Jansens were prosecuted for slander, for incurring debt, for not paying wages to an employee, and "for injury caused to the plaintiff's hog by the defendant's dog." These were issues that arose largely from personal confrontation. They seem trivial to us today but they constituted major legal issues in that rough-and-tumble settlement.

Of Crime & Punishment

BESIDES BEING FINED, convicted offenders were often given jail sentences, but since the colony had no prison, the guilty usually served out their sentences at home. One offender, François de Bruyn, was fined 200 guilders for insulting and striking a court messenger. He refused to pay up, whereupon he was ordered to be imprisoned "in a respectable tavern," surely a sentence he must not have found all that unbearable. At last, the colony acquired a Stadt Huys or city hall in the form of a house originally built by Kieft as a tavern. The court met in the spacious former taproom, while the smaller rooms and storage spaces in the building were converted to prison cells.

The usual penalty for stealing was scourging with rods, often followed by banishment from the colony for a stated period of time. A man found guilty of a more serious offense might have an ear cut off before being permanently banished. And the ultimate punishment was death by "the cord," that is, by hanging.

In 1641 there was an unsuccessful attempt at hanging that left a deep impression on the hundreds of people who witnessed it. Nine slaves had jointly confessed to the murder of another slave and were told to draw lots to determine which one should pay for the crime. The lot fell on Manuel Gerrit, nicknamed the Giant. Four days later Gerrit took his place atop a ladder, propped against a wall of the Fort, with two strong halters around his neck. The ladder was pulled away, Gerrit thrashed frantically in the air, and under the strain of his struggling and enormous weight *both* halters broke, and the huge black man plummeted to the ground. On his knees, crying out in some African tongue, he pulled at the grass and pounded on the ground. Women screamed, and men quickly joined the slave's obvious prayer for mercy. Meanwhile, the hooded hangman prepared a stronger rope, but as he walked with it toward the prisoner a mighty cry went up from the crowd. Kieft, obviously fearing what might happen, relented, and the giant was quietly led from the scene by fellow slaves.

Soldiers and sailors suffered their own brands of refined punishment. Soldiers convicted of rioting or drunkenness were made to "ride the wooden horse," a carpenter's sawhorse about twelve feet high standing between Pearl Street and the Fort, with a weight tied to each ankle. Sailors were punished by being pushed three times from the yardarm and each time they landed on the deck, receiving a well-aimed kick from their shipmates.

In New Amsterdam, where public entertainment of a more uplifting nature was rarely available, such spectacles drew large audiences. The court sessions were well-attended, too, and the citizens of New Amsterdam were unquestionably better acquainted with court routine and the workings of the judicial system than most New Yorkers are today.

Stuyvesant Versus The Rest

PETER STUYVESANT, welcomed to New Amsterdam with high hopes and much goodwill after the departure of the unlamented Kieft, soon revealed himself to be an autocrat, with a narrow outlook and rigorously orthodox views. But Stuyvesant was, most of all, a loyal servant of the West India Company. Indeed, so loyal that when the directors ordered him to stop persecuting Quakers and to allow Jews to enter New Netherland, he quickly reversed himself and did his best to implement a policy of tolerance which he, personally, found intolerable.

The new director general had barely settled into his new post when popular pressure forced him to accept an advisory body known as the Nine Men in his council. These men represented the three groups that contributed most to the colony's wealth: the merchants, the burghers and the farmers. Three men from each class were selected by the heads of the leading families. Three of the Nine, one from each group, attended court when civil cases were being tried and, when called upon, acted as arbitrators. As such, they constituted the beginnings of an elected judiciary.

While the *schout* had always played the leading role in court, there had also been room for skilled pleaders, mostly clerks and notaries, sometimes dignified by the title of attorney. But now, with the three representatives from the Nine Men acting as arbitrators, there was less need for their services. Meanwhile, the Nine Men became an important factor in provincial government. Stuyvesant, resenting their power, bided his time. In 1651, when they had the audacity to complain of his arbitrariness to the directors of the Dutch West India Company, he dismissed them. But instead of clearing the air, this move simply increased the popular clamor for reform. Pleas and petitions went off to the company directors, and even to the Netherlands' governing body, the States General. The States General ordered Stuyvesant to step down, but goaded on by the Dutch West India Company, he refused, saying, "I shall do as I please." However, a year later, the Dutch government decided to curb the ram-

bunctious company and its director general, and ordered Stuyvesant to give New Amsterdam a so-called burgher government,
raising it to an equal status with the largely self-governing cities
and towns at home.

Chosen in two successive steps—first by their peers in an election and then by Stuyvesant—the new officials took office early
the following year as the very first municipal government any-
where in what is now the United States. Two of them were
burgomasters and five were schepens, a schepen being roughly
equivalent to an alderman. They constituted, with the *schout,* a
court with both civil and criminal jurisdiction; called, variously,
the Court of Burgomasters and Schepens and the Schepens'
Court. The judges of this court were the first in the colony to
have any degree of independence from the Dutch West India
Company. In contrast to his earlier arrogance, Stuyvesant now
addressed the court as "Honourable, Beloved, Faithful, The
Schout, Burgomasters and Schepens." A far cry from "I shall do
as I please." The court met once a week at the Stadt Huys, and
would continue to function, under a different name, until 1895,
when it was absorbed by the New York State Supreme Court.

A large segment of New Netherland society remained outside
the control of the company. This was the feudal patroon system
which flourished in the Hudson Valley. In their domain, patroons were the omnipotent authority. Colonists were required
to obtain the patroon's written consent before leaving his shire.
Like the serfs of the Middle Ages, they were bound to the land.
They bought or bartered everything at the patroon's store and a
portion of their crops was paid as rent each year. Patroons administered justice, often according to their whims. Van Renssae-
ler exacted a promise from his colonists not to appeal any of his
judicial decisions to Holland. In essence this gave him absolute
power; it also served to weaken the authority and prestige of the
West India Company.

In 1654, when a census showed 120 houses and about 1,000
people in New Amsterdam, the magistrates were given the
power to levy taxes and convey lands. A painted coat of arms, a
seal and a silver signet were delivered to them with great cere-

mony. But Stuyvesant was not prepared to share power with these creatures of the fickle and unstable electorate. "We derive our authority," he declared, "from God and the West India Company, not from the pleasure of a few ignorant subjects."

Nevertheless, with the support of the directors in Amsterdam, the power of the magistrates continued to expand. In 1657 burgher rights were granted, which meant that no merchant could thereafter do business and no craftsman ply his trade without first being admitted by the magistrates to the freedom of the city. In 1658 the magistrates won the right to nominate their successors. And in 1660 the company further raised the prestige of the *schout* by relieving him of his burdensome duties as sheriff, prosecutor and presiding magistrate. One man could no longer, in any case, handle so many jobs, for New Amsterdam had trebled in size during the 1650's and now contained some 350 houses and more than 3,000 people.

Even as the magistrates waxed more powerful, challenging the director general's supremacy and functioning as a counterweight to him in the control of the town's affairs, that beleaguered band, lawyers, was subjected to still more restrictions: in 1658 fees for legal services were fixed at a modest level, and lawyers were obligated to provide such services free to the poor.

New Netherland Becomes New York

For Years, most acutely during the Anglo-Dutch War of 1652-54, Stuyvesant and his councilors had worried that the English settlers east of New Netherland might one day invade their colony. The growth of English towns on Long Island also caused them anxiety. So did the infiltration of Yankee farmers from Connecticut and Massachusetts. Meanwhile, in New Amsterdam itself, the English had become so numerous that some were elected schepens. Now the most active notary-practitioner-pleader-lawyers owed their prosperity to their fluency in both Dutch and English.

In 1664 the worldwide struggle between England and Holland for commercial and maritime supremacy again broke out in war. Stuyvesant appealed to the Dutch West India Company for arms and reinforcements, but before these could arrive an English fleet appeared in the upper bay off New Amsterdam. Its commander, Colonel Richard Nicolls, called on Stuyvesant to surrender, and the Dutchman did so, realizing that resistance against the formidable English guns would be doomed to fail. So, "without the shedding of a drop of blood or a tear," Dutch New Amsterdam became English New York, renamed in honor of the town's owner, the Duke of York.

Stuyvesant sailed to Holland to personally give to the States General his reasons for giving up the colony without a fight. He returned to New York almost immediately and retired to his *bouwerie,* or farm, dying there in 1672.

Nicolls set about reorganizing the colony along English lines. The first constitution of the colony of New York consisted of four documents: the king's patent granting it to the duke, the duke's commission naming Nicolls his governor, a proclamation by Nicolls asserting the duke's authority over the English settlers on Long Island, and the Dutch articles of capitulation. The first document was, of course, the most important, as it provided the royal authorization on which all the rest was based. It bound the duke to make no law that did not harmonize with the laws of England, and empowered him to establish courts founded on the English system.

English Laws, Dutch Practices

In Orderly fashion, Nicolls set about following his instructions. He established a local court in each town to try civil suits involving five pounds or less, and a Court of Sessions with jurisdiction over suits involving more than five pounds. This court also dealt with criminal cases. Its decisions could be appealed to the province's highest tribunal, the Court of Assize, composed of the governor and his council together with the magistrates of the several towns. In the City of New York, Nicolls refashioned the

Schepens' Court into the Mayor's Court, and when he appointed new judges to it, he was diplomatic enough to include several leading Dutchmen. He next introduced trial by jury, and on June 27,1665 the first jury in New York's history was empaneled.

In October of that same year, Ralph Hall and his wife were tried in the Court of Assize for "bewitching" George Wood and his daughter. A portion of the indictment read:

[The accused] by some detestable and wicked arts, commonly called witch craft and sorcery, did maliciously practice and exercise at the said town of Seatalcott, etc., on the person of George Wood, late of that same place, by which wicked and detestable arts, the said George Wood most dangerously and mortally sickened and languished, and not long after, by the aforesaid wicked and detestable arts, the said George Wood died.

Hall and his wife pleaded not guilty and, as there were no witnesses against them, they were acquitted and released on "good behavior." This occurred some twenty-six years before the famed Salem witch trials of 1691 and 1692, earning New York a dubious first in America's legal history.

With the international trade New York enjoyed as a result of its change of masters, the city prospered and its population burgeoned. By 1667, when Anglo-Dutch hostilities officially ended, it boasted some 8,000 people. That year, Nicolls resigned as governor and returned to England. He was killed in action five years later in the opening phase of the third and last Anglo-Dutch War. In the course of that conflict, a Dutch naval force recaptured New York. For eighteen months in 1673 and 1674, the city, this time rechristened New Orange, once again lived under Dutch rule and Dutch law. The terms of the peace treaty ending the war returned the city to English rule, and it became the property, as before, of the Duke of York.

On the surface, the reformation of the judicial system and institutions Nicolls carried out was very thorough, but beneath that surface much remained the same: arbitration, which had been so important in New Netherland, continued to be important in New York under the Duke's Laws. The traditions of Dutch civil law also remained. As one scholar puts it, "cases were still decided on the basis of general, theoretical rules of justice rather than according to empirical, historical precedents of Common Law." Examination of court records from the first three decades of English rule reveals a general ignorance of, or perhaps indifference to, the English Common Law, together with a marked lack of sophistication in the drafting of legal documents. Law was still a matter of simple ethics and justice rather than legal precedents, which meant that when it came to representing clients in court, notaries and clerks were as able as full-time lawyers, and distinctly preferred to them.

For in the colony and city of New York, a frontier with frontier values, suspicion of the legal fraternity ran as deep among the English as it had among the Dutch.

Unrest & Upheaval

AFTER NICOLLS, New Yorkers suffered through seven unhappy years (1674-81) under Sir Edmund Andros, who earned their dislike with his high-handed ways. His successor, Thomas Dongan, was a very different man and much more popular. In 1683, on the Duke of York's instructions, Dongan called a legislative assembly which passed measures known as the Charter of Liberties and Privileges granting popular rights and religious tolerance. It was the first "Bill of Rights" for New Yorkers. Dongan also revamped the court system, abolishing the Court of Assize and splitting its functions between a two-justice Court of Oyer and Terminer and a Court of Chancery composed of his council and himself. In addition, a petty court was established for each town and a court of common pleas for each county.

When the king of England died in 1685 the Duke, who was his brother, succeeded him as James II. Although James did not approve Dongan's reforms, they were continued, because of the Charter of Liberties and Privileges which Dongan had contrived. In 1686, James made the hated Andros governor of all

41

Thomas Donegan, a royal governor who encouraged religious tolerance and the granting of some rights to the common citizen.

New England, and in 1688 put him in charge of New York as well, with Francis Nicholson his deputy there. Early the following year, however, the colonists heard the electrifying news of the "Glorious Revolution." Catholic James had been dethroned and replaced by his Protestant daughter Mary and her Dutch husband, William, Prince of Orange. In Boston, the people rose against Andros and clapped him in jail. And in New York there began the dramatic sequence of events known as the Leisler Rebellion.

Rumor circulated throughout the colony that the French were preparing to invade from Canada to avenge the dethroning of their fellow Catholic, King James. Jacob Leisler sounded the call for Protestant resistance. With the aid of the militia, which he headed, Leisler took control of the city and proclaimed William and Mary the new sovereigns, and himself royal governor.

In time, the council at Albany recognized Leisler's authority, although the colonial aristocracy bitterly opposed and feared him. Meanwhile, in London William and Mary appointed Colonel Henry Sloughter the royal governor. Leisler continued to hold the fort on Manhattan, refusing to believe the stories that a new governor was on the way from England. Fighting broke out, but when Sloughter actually arrived, Leisler immediately surrendered. He was put under arrest and indicted first for treason and then for murder, since a man had been killed during the skirmish over the fort. Leisler was speedily convicted and sentenced to be hanged.

Even at the time of his trial, some of Leisler's most implacable foes recognized that his conviction had been a travesty of justice. Four years later Parliament was to reverse the verdict against him and voted to indemnify his heirs. Leisler's execution gave the believers in popular government a martyr. His memory would be invoked by them for decades in their political tug-of-war with the colony's landed aristocrats and merchant princes. But if the trial of Jacob Leisler is a particularly conspicuous blot on the record of unbiased justice in New York, it can also be seen as a turning point, the end of a rude era when law and justice were tailored to suit the needs of the moment.

The Dongan court system lasted until 1691 when Colonel Henry Sloughter, the new governor, authorized the convening of a "General Assembly of Freeholders." This assembly established a new court system and created a blueprint for county government that lasts, in part, to this very day.

Sloughter's county government system included the election of town supervisors by qualified voters and the creation of the elected office of county treasurer. This "supervisor system" of county government was used as a model for western settlements, making New York the originator of this sort of government in America.

The Sloughter Assembly created a judicial system that included a high Court of Chancery composed, of course, of the Governor and his Council, a Supreme Court, County Courts (Courts of Mayors and Aldermen) and on the local level, small courts of justices of the peace. The Supreme Court was the most interesting creation of the Sloughter Assembly because our present court strongly resembles it. The court consisted of a chief justice and four associate (puisne) justices. A quorum consisted of the chief justice and two associates. The court had jurisdiction over civil and criminal cases. In civil judgments exceeding five hundred pounds, an appeal to the king was possible.

Following the cases the New York Supreme Court heard and the decisions it made is like reading a political and social history of the colony for eighty-five years before the Declaration of Independence. Actually the Supreme Court served as a forum for the fights between New Yorkers and the king concerning who should govern in the colony. Unlike the other colonies where the king gave this right by charter to the people, New York was ruled by royal prerogative. Until the Revolution no longer made it necessary, New York lawyers fought tirelessly to rid the colony of this prerogative. On days when these "agitating attorneys" were to try a case, crowds would assemble in the court, eagerly cheering on their champions. Indeed, the Supreme Court often resembled a corner in London's Hyde Park, with lawyers becoming orators, the crowds responding hysterically. It is extraordinary to realize that the political sentiments of the colony were shouted out in, of all places, the halls of the New York Supreme Court.

Arguments were continually flaring up between the colonial legislatures and governors about who would be appointed to the court. The governors wanted outsiders, non-New Yorkers, as justices. Such judges, they reasoned, would owe allegiance to royal authority, not to a New York political faction. On the other hand, the legislatures always backed New York lawyers or judges. Lieutenant-Governor Cadwallader Colden expressed how his side felt in a letter to the Lords of Trade in 1761. Colden argued:

If then a chief justice for life, with large family connections, form a party, to serve ambitions or interested views, the governor must either become the tool of this party or live in perpetual contention.

Soon after this, Colden became involved in a heated dispute with New York lawyers and the Supreme Court. In 1764, Colden, a fierce believer in royal supremacy, allowed Waddell Cunningham, who had lost a case before the court, to appeal to the governor. Before this, appeals were allowed only for "writ of error" (mistrial). The Cunningham case had no writ of error. The legislature, lawyers, and the common people hotly protested Colden's attempt to give the governor powers that clearly belonged to the court. He was forced to retract his move. The New York Assembly deemed the act a "mischievous Innovation." It was said of Colden, "the old Body was always disliked enough, but now they [the people] would prefer Beelzebub himself to him."

By 1710, all remnants of Dutch legal institutions were abolished and New York's court system was based on the English, with Common Law recognized as the law of the colony. It was far from a harmonious judiciary. The courtroom became the arena for colonial protest, a stage for lawyer and client speaking out against the crown. Leading the dissent were New York attorneys who, as we know, had recently banded together in the first informal bar association.

This, then, was the scene in colonial New York, when John Peter Zenger, publisher of the *New York Weekly Journal,* went on trial in 1735 for libeling the governor. It is probably the most renowned case in New York legal history.

The Zenger Case

The Liberty of the Press is a Subject of the greatest importance, and in which every Individual is as much concerned as he is in any other Part of Liberty.—John Peter Zenger, *The New York Weekly Journal,* November 12, 1733

JOHN PETER ZENGER became publisher of the *New York Weekly Journal* in 1733 to oppose the *New York Gazette* which backed the policies of Governor Cosby. The newspaper was financed by several prominent lawyers and merchants—all opposed to rule by royal prerogative in New York. It has been claimed by many historians that Zenger, a German immigrant, was being used by these men. The fact remains that the *New York Weekly Journal* published, in blistering rhetoric, attacks against the royal Governor, William Cosby, and that the popular newspaper reflected the strong opposition to royal authority in New York.

The paper's attacks, some in the form of satiric ballads, infuriated Cosby. The governor ordered that the newspaper "be burnt by the common hangman." The colonial assembly ignored Cosby's demand that a reward be offered for the arrest of the author of these "libels." With that, Cosby turned to his own considerable powers.

Zenger was arrested through an order of Cosby's Council. The publisher's influential friends did not put up bail, hoping that Zenger would assume the mantle of a martyr to the man in the street. He was indicted for "false, scandalous, malicious and seditious" libels, but the governor was foiled by the grand jury when it refused to indict Zenger. Furious at this snub, Cosby directed his attorney general to file suit against Zenger and made certain that the trial took place before his puppet judges, headed by Chief Justice James DeLancey of the Supreme Court. Zenger's lawyers, led by James Alexander and William Smith, strongly protested. DeLancey disbarred both men, citing contempt as the reason. In effect, Zenger was stripped of any legal aid.

Smith and Alexander realized that it would be necessary to look for attorneys outside of New York. They turned to Philadelphia where they enlisted the help of the celebrated lawyer, Andrew Hamilton, for Zenger's defense. John Chambers agreed to become the publisher's assistant defense counsel. Hamilton conducted Zenger's defense brilliantly. His arguments were so persuasive and eloquent that they were widely published in England as well as America. The aged attorney spoke of his dedication to the principle of independence of the press and the obligations of the legal profession in his argument to the jury:

You see I labor under the weight of many years, and am borne down with great infirmities of body. Yet old and weak as I am, I should think it my duty, if required, to go to the utmost part of the land, where my service could be of any use in a system to quench the flame of prosecutions upon informations, set afoot by the government, to deprive a people of the right of remonstrating, and complaining of the arbitrary attempts of men in power.

Hamilton argued that if what Zenger printed in his newspaper was indeed true, then it could not be considered libelous. Chambers, echoing Hamilton, made the point that criticism of a government could never be considered libel, if it were truthful in nature. Chambers went on to compare Cosby's tactics to those of the hated British Star Chamber Court.

Chief Justice DeLancey instructed the jury not to consider whether what Zenger printed was truthful or not, but simply to confirm or deny that libel was committed. It was the judge's task, he contended, to determine whether the libel was the truth or a falsehood. DeLancey's warning words were of no avail. The jury took little time in reaching a verdict. The words "not guilty" were greeted with shouts and cheers. Horsemen and runners took news of the verdict to all parts of the colony. But even in their vast enthusiasm, the jubilant crowds could hardly have realized the importance of the verdict—for it established that if a written statement is true it cannot be called libel, thereby giving the press freedom to criticize the actions of the government.

Hamilton was the hero of the day. New York held a ball in his honor and the city's common council gave him a gold box, symbol of the "freedom of the city." Upon leaving, Hamilton was taken to his waiting barge with the pomp and ceremony usually reserved for royalty or the loftiest of dignitaries. Zenger, of course, had been released from prison and immediately returned to his paper to continue writing his telling revelations about the governor. How that must have stung the arrogant Cosby!

And so it was that two courageous New York lawyers flouted royal authority and along with two other resolute attorneys changed the entire course of American history by insuring freedom of the press.

The Later Colonial Era
Through The Revolution

AMERICAN CULTURE, during the colonial era, imitated the British. In drama, for example, American playwrights copied English Restoration satire, and English plays filled the few theaters that existed in New York, Boston and Philadelphia. So it was with the law. During the colonial period, American law was based on English Common Law and its courts were replicas of the British. Julius Goebel, in his "The Courts and the Law" chapter in *History of the State of New York,* writes that New York law at that time was a "mere parasite grafted onto the law of England." The era of innovation and "Americanizing" was to come later. English Common Law was still the focus of America's legal thought.

The lawyers of the New York colony were another thing. Writing to the Earl of Halifax, Lieutenant Governor Colden berated colonial lawyers:

The dangerous influence which the profession of law has obtained in this province, more than any other part of his Majesty's dominions, is a principal cause of disputing appeals to the King.

In the *History of the Bench and Bar of New York,* Colden's accusation is substantiated:

It was a frequent taunt in ministerial circles at Westminster that the whole unfortunate trouble from the Stamp Act down to the Declaration was an affair of the colonial lawyers.

Certainly both statements exaggerate, but they do illustrate how lawyers, using the New York colonial courts as a stage, played a major role in encouraging dissatisfaction and rebellion in the colony.

And, even more important, this irksome profession rapidly grew in America. Edmund Burke, famed British politician, kept an interested eye on New York and watched the enormous interest in the law grow even greater. He said:

In no country perhaps in the world is the law so general a study. The profession itself is numerous and powerful; and in most provinces it takes the lead. The greater number of deputies sent to Congress were lawyers. But all who read—and most do read —endeavor to obtain some smattering of that science.

Burke also observed that Blackstone's *Commentaries* sold nearly as many copies in America as it did in England!

During the Revolution, the courts were in disarray. After the British captured the city, General Howe closed all New York courts, though they had been functioning while Washington held the city. In the courts that remained open in other parts of the colony, loyalist justices ruled. Patriots, and those suspected of harboring patriot sympathies, received harsh treatment. The plundering by British soldiers, their mercenaries, Indians and loyalists often went without prosecution. New York was under martial law. The gravity of the situation is shown in this vivid description of the appointment, in 1780, of William Smith as Chief Justice of the Supreme Court: "at a time when no law but military and police law existed, when not a court of justice under the jurisdiction of Britain was open and when there was no more occasion for a Chief Justice than there was for a Bishop or a Pope."

All was not fighting and destruction. Some men looked to the future when, in spite of the fear and indecision, they were certain the colony would be a colony no more. Determined to rule themselves and rule by law, these confident and optimistic men held a constitutional convention in 1776. The moving spirit behind this step was John Jay, a youthful attorney of extraordinary ability and vision. With the help of Robert Livingston and Gouverneur Morris, Jay drafted a constitution at a time when the colony was in chaos. Of the difficulties he faced, Jay wrote:

We have a government to form and God knows what it will resemble — our politicians, like some guests at a feast, are perplexed and undetermined which dish to prefer.

He had a sense of humor as well.

The convention met first at White Plains on July 9, 1776 and

John Jay, drafter of the first New York State constitution, Governor of New York and the first Chief Justice of the United States Supreme Court.

then at Kingston where, on April 20, 1777, the constitution was adopted by a vote of thirty-two to one. Two days later the document was read publicly from the steps of the Kingston Court House.

Among the items included in the remarkable constitution were the following:

1. A separation of power among the executive, legislative and judicial branches of government.

2. Popular election of the governor.

3. A bicameral legislature consisting of the Senate and the Assembly.

4. Maintenance of established courts and the British Common Law.

5. Property qualifications for voting. (This item shows the influence of Jay, a man who later became a strong "Federalist" on the American government.)

6. Guarantees of freedom of religion and jury trial.

Alexander Hamilton said of the constitution, "I think your Government far the best we have yet seen and capable of giving long and substantial happiness to the people." Hamilton was correct, and New York's first constitution became the model for other state constitutions. Perhaps most notable of all is the fact that the major provisions of Jay's document live to this day in the federal and state constitutions.

No bells rang, no gala celebrations marked the announcement of the constitution's ratification. This was a troubled time in New York and it is remarkable that progress of such magnitude could have been achieved at all.

Beginnings of
an American Legal System
in New York

In the formative era of American law, the aim of the lawmakers was practical, not abstract justice. —Bernard Schwartz, *Law in America*

WITH THE coming of peace a new jurisprudence developed, "American" in its departure from its British foundations. America's first great legal writer, James Kent of New York, was influential in steering lawyers away from the tradition-bound Common Law. William E. Nelson, in *Americanization of the Common Law*, writes that the period from 1780 to 1820 witnessed two major changes in this nation's judiciary: a change in the roles of judges and juries when it came to determining the law and the facts relevant to a case; and the interpretation of laws to suit an ever changing American society, replacing the precedence of rigid adherence to Common Law. The phrase "a changing law for changing times" and Schwartz's quotation about "practical, not abstract justice" really best describe the American adaptation of Common Law.

In the colonial and post-Revolutionary era it was generally agreed that judges should avoid loose interpretation of law and should apply Common Law precedent at all times. The jury tried to find the statute that best suited the relevant facts of the particular case. In the Zenger case, when the jury ignored Justice DeLancey's charge, they did so because the law and the facts made it obvious they must do so. The values of the community played a large part in determining law. A relatively homogeneous community would naturally incorporate its values into each jury's verdict. Within the bounds of English law, the jury could "find" the law, sift through the facts, and reach a verdict. The Zenger case exemplifies the influence of community values on the law. Looking at the jury's action and decision, it is easy to figure out how the community and the colony felt about Governor Cosby.

The new, Americanized Common Law increased the importance of judges and allowed a flexible interpretation of the law. As Chief Justice Isaac Parker of the Massachusetts Supreme Court explained:

[The] principles of common law [would] undoubtedly apply at all times, the application of these principles may be different now, from that which was made several hundred years ago, when the rule was laid down.

As juries relinquished their authority to state that a certain law was applicable to the case, judges began to take over that role. A judge had the power to interpret the law as he saw fit or as changing times and conditions dictated. As time went on, judges began the practice of writing their opinions, so their interpretation of a specific law could be studied and understood. English Common Law precedent was discarded and replaced by its American adaptation, expressed in these written opinions which were widely circulated and influenced law throughout the country. The great collage of these opinions, recorded through the years, has become the law we know today.

Lawyers & the Law: Profiles of Five New York Legal Figures

NEW YORK has known many able practitioners of law. Alexander Hamilton, the Van Burens, John Jay, William Seward and Charles Evans Hughes are names that even schoolboys recognize. Less widely known, but no less important in their contribution to New York legal history, are James Kent, Robert Livingston, William Evarts, Joseph Choate and Benjamin Cardozo. These giants of their profession left us a legacy that merits study today.

JAMES KENT, THE "AMERICAN BLACKSTONE" In 1823, United States Supreme Court Justice Joseph Story toasted James Kent as "our distinguished guest, who so administered the law of the land as to make New York the land of the law." Justice Story's tribute has been echoed and re-echoed throughout history in recognition of Kent's great influence in the development of American law. Indeed, James Kent could have proved Thomas Carlyle's statement that history is the saga of great men and their contributions to civilization. Kent so influenced the legal profession during his lifetime that those years have been deemed the "golden period of New York law."

James Kent was born in Dutchess County in 1763, of a blue-blooded Connecticut Yankee family. Elisha Kent, the patriarch of the family, was his grandfather. Moss Kent, James' father, was the eldest of Elisha's children. The Kents were socially prominent, well-educated people. Elisha was a Presbyterian clergyman who devoted much of his life to organizing the church in Dutchess County. Moss studied law under Lieutenant Governor Thomas Fitch of Connecticut. He was admitted to the New York bar at Poughkeepsie in 1755. James Kent, his father and grandfather were all graduates of Yale, and mixed socially with the aristocrats of Connecticut and New York. Kent's manner left no doubt that he considered himself born to the purple.

*James Kent, the judge who established the tradition of written opinions,
thereby creating the base for the American version of British Common Law.*

After graduating from Yale, Kent took his legal training with
New York Attorney General Egbert Benson. Benson was a particularly good choice for Kent. The attorney general was acquainted with most of the important New Yorkers and, through
his legal expertise and political position, profoundly influenced
the State Supreme Court. Under Benson's guidance, Kent was
admitted to the New York bar in January 1785.

Kent's aristocratic leanings made him sympathetic to the Federalist Party. He was a close friend of Alexander Hamilton's and
eventually became a Federalist representative in the state Assembly. Kent's career as a judge began in relative obscurity as a
circuit justice for western New York. John T. Horton, in his
article, "The Western Eyres of Judge Kent" (*New York History*,
April, 1937) commented on Kent's circuit justice role:

In availing himself of his opportunity to make the oracles of
Westminster Hall re-echo through the country of the Genesee,
Kent laid the foundation for that fame which moved Mr. Justice
Story to extoll him.

But life on the western New York circuit was not to Kent's liking. At the end of the eighteenth century this area was a frontier wilderness. Few roads existed and water transportation was used whenever possible. Harsh climate, rugged countryside, disease and the solitude of the great forests plagued all those who traveled. The world of the western New York frontier was far from what James Kent had been accustomed to.

Kent compensated for his isolation and discomfort by seeking out the few educated, landed settlers of the region. He spent many evenings with Thomas Morris of Canandaigua, John Lincklaen of Cazenovia, and Charles Williamson, the agent of the Holland Land Company, at Bath. The justice did not relish having to deal with frontier folk who, he believed, were too "democratic" in their outlook.Again, we see the haughty aristocrat in this opinion of Kent.

On December 24, 1793, Kent was appointed to a law professorship at Columbia. He relinquished his university chair when Governor John Jay appointed him to the State Supreme Court. Kent became a "puisne," or associate justice. In 1804 he became Chief Justice and, in 1814, Chancellor of New York, administering the Court of Chancery, a relic of British times. Kent remained Chancellor until he retired in 1823 at the age of sixty. He then resumed his professorship at Columbia, during which time he gave a series of lectures on American law. These lectures were later compiled in Kent's famous *Commentaries on American Law,* the first authoritative work on that subject.

In an 1828 letter to his friend Thomas Washington, Kent discussed his work as a State Supreme Court Justice:

When I came to the bench there were no reports or state precedents. The opinions of the bench were delivered *ore tenus.* We had no law of our own and nobody knew what it was. I first introduced a thorough examination of cases and written opinions. [The decision in the 1799 case of] "Ludlow v. Dale" is a sample of the earliest [written opinion]. The judges, when we met, all assumed that foreign sentences were only good *prima facie.* I presented and read my written opinion that they were conclusive, and they all gave up to me, and so I read it in court as it now stands. This was the commencement of a new plan, and then was laid the first stone in the subsequently erected temple of our jurisprudence.

It has been said that Kent's written opinions gave us our precedents, and our bench and bar then "began to walk independently" of English law. Kent expanded on the newly developed role of the judge in America and used that role to begin the designing of an American version of English Common Law.

The Supreme Court reporters contributed enormously to the rise of judges like James Kent. These men recorded the cases and the opinions of the judges. Their work insured that significant opinions and precedents would be circulated throughout America. The first New York State Supreme Court reporter was George Gaines, appointed in 1804. William Johnson, Gaines' successor, compiled descriptions of important legal cases in his book *Cases* which was widely circulated.

No one man has contributed more to New York's legal system than James Kent. His work on the Supreme Court and his *Commentaries* brought about a major shift in the focus of American law. The written opinion became custom. It reflected a new trend in our jurisprudence and served as a flexible departure from strict Common Law precedent. When examined closely, the opinion mirrored the thinking of the times.

Kent, the originator of the written opinion, the chronicler of American law, the circuit justice, the Supreme Court judge, the professor of law at Columbia, most certainly earned his title, "The American Blackstone."

ROBERT R. LIVINGSTON was born in New York City on November 11, 1746. He became one of New York's most distinguished lawyers. Livingston was of patriotic, patrician stock. His father, Robert, was a lawyer and judge in New York colony and one of the old Hudson Valley landed gentry. The older Livingston, as a member of the Stamp Act Congress, wrote the official protest to the king. Because of his opposition to colonial taxation, Livingston senior was disbarred in 1774.

Robert Livingston

The younger Livingston received the customary education of one of his class. At Kings College (now Columbia University) Livingston was a classmate of John Jay's. At their commencement in 1764, Jay gave a speech about "peace" and Livingston gave one about "liberty." Livingston's oration so moved the reporters of the *New York Gazette* that they wrote "the young orator may prove an able and zealous asserter, and defender, of the rights and liberties of his country." After graduation Livingston studied law with William Smith and was admitted to the bar in October, 1773.

Livingston's career of public service began soon after his becoming an attorney. A member of the Second Continental Congress, Livingston, along with Jefferson, John Adams, Franklin and Roger Sherman, was selected to draft the Declaration of Independence. Oddly enough Livingston did not sign that historic document. He was not present at the ceremony because he had been recalled to New York to assist Jay in framing our state's first independent government.

In 1777 Livingston accepted an appointment as Chancellor of New York. At that time, it was a thankless job. The Court of

Chancery was under attack from many New Yorkers because no jury was involved in its decisions. People had come to regard the court as an anti-democratic British leftover. Livingston's performance, however, did much to change that sentiment. The Chancery Reports, written some fifteen years later when Kent was Chancellor, contained the following reference to Livingston:

It has been said that 'this august tribunal never boasted a more prompt, more able or more faithful officer than Chancellor Livingston.'

Sadly, there were no written Chancery Reports during the time Livingston held office.

The Chancellor resigned his post in 1801 when Jefferson appointed him American minister to France. In this role Robert Livingston made his greatest contribution to his country. Largely through his work, a treaty between the United States and France was negotiated and signed in 1803 and resulted in the Louisiana Purchase. Napoleon was willing to cede the territory to America because he felt that a strong America would rival England as a maritime power—all to the good, as far as France was concerned.

Livingston's thoughts on the matter echoed Bonaparte's optimism:

We have lived long, but this is the noblest work of our whole lives. The treaty which we have just signed has not been obtained by art or dictated by force. Equally advantageous to the two contracting parties, it will change vast solitudes into flourishing districts; from this day the United States take their place among the powers of first rank.

Many years before, at Washington's inauguration, Livingston had declared, "Long live George Washington, President of the United States." Had the first President lived to pay eulogy to Livingston when he died on February 26, 1813, he undoubtedly would have voiced similar sentiments about this illustrious member of the New York Bar.

WILLIAM MAXWELL EVARTS was a "lawyer's lawyer," who did what he thought was right, regardless of personal gain or public opinion. He stands as one of New York's greatest attorneys, a man whose brilliant career has been a beacon to many who followed him.

Cardinal Wolsey once stated that in a political case a jury would, if necessary, bring in a verdict that Abel killed Cain.—William Maxwell Evarts, in defense of Andrew Johnson

Evarts was born in Boston and educated at the prestigious Boston Latin School. He graduated from Yale in 1837, and for a while, taught school in Vermont. Then Evarts entered Harvard Law School and, after graduation, he was accepted at Daniel Lord's law office in New York City as a clerk.

Evarts learned a great deal about practical politics during his early years in New York. He backed first Whigs and then Republicans at city ward meetings, and eventually became close friends with New York's Republican kingpin, William Seward. At the 1860 Republican National Convention, Evarts led the unsuccessful pro-Seward delegation. Evarts' political and professional career received a boost when Millard Fillmore became President. Fillmore, a New Yorker from Buffalo, appointed Evarts Assistant District Attorney of New York.

The first major trial in which Evarts distinguished himself was the Lemmon Case in 1860. This case involved Juliet Lemmon, her husband, and eight slaves, who stopped in New York on the way to Texas. While in the city the Lemmons were served with a writ of *habeas corpus,* charging that their slaves were being deprived of due liberty. Evarts prosecuted this case, arguing that New York's anti-slavery laws automatically freed blacks whenever they entered the state. Opposing Evarts and representing the Lemmons and the sanctity of property rights, was Charles O'Conor, a prominent lawyer of the New York bar. Evarts won the case, receiving a five to three vote in the Court of Appeals. Most of his arguments sustained every challenge by O'Conor.

Certainly William Evarts' finest hour was the defense of Andrew Johnson at his impeachment trial. As a member of the

William Evarts

defense team, Evarts' duties consisted of cross-examining witnesses, presenting arguments upon evidence, and making a pri-
mary summation. Evarts' closing address was masterful. These
are some of the words that rang out in the Senate, echoing in
many a hostile ear:

If, indeed, our closely cinctured liberty, is at last to loosen her
zone, and her stern monitor, law, debauched and drunken with
this new wine of opinion that is crushing daily from ten thou-
sand presses throughout the land, is to withdraw its guardian-
ship, let us be counted with those who, with averted eye and
reverent step backward, seek to veil this shameless revelry, and
not with those who exult and cheer at its excesses.

Evarts' success in the Johnson impeachment case brought a well-
earned reward—the nomination and confirmation as United
States Attorney General.

Evarts later distinguished himself as representative of the
United States at the Geneva Tribunal in 1871, which was consid-
ering American claims against the *Alabama*. The *Alabama* was a
Confederate raider, outfitted by the English. Because of Evarts'

efforts, the United States won a damage judgment against England of fifteen million dollars, to compensate for losses attributed to the *Alabama* during the Civil War. This was a landmark victory in international law.

Evarts was not content to stop. He became the first president of the Bar Association of the City of New York and was a leader in the fight against the Tweed Ring. He successfully represented Rutherford B. Hayes in 1877 before the United States Electoral Commission and was subsequently made Secretary of State by Hayes when he became President. In 1885 Evarts was elected to the United States Senate.

An observer of Evarts' career once commented:

Had Evarts performed services of similar magnitude for private clients, his fees would have been princely, nor would he then have incurred the risk which shadowed him throughout and after the Impeachment Trial, of party ostracism and hatred.

But risk did not bother William Maxwell Evarts.

JOSEPH HODGES CHOATE, like his friend and contemporary Evarts, was a New Englander by birth. A native of Salem, Massachusetts, Choate was born on January 24, 1832, and graduated from both Harvard and Harvard Law School. He worked for a year in the Boston law office of Leverett Saltonstall before being admitted to the Massachusetts Bar in 1855. Later that same year, he made his last and permanent move to New York City and was soon admitted to the New York Bar. In 1859 he joined the firm of Evarts, Southmayd and Choate, where he worked for the rest of his life.

He was the delight of juries who yielded gladly to his charm and the pride of courts who felt the dignity of their office enhanced by his appearance before them.—Elihu Root, in a memorial to Joseph Choate

---

Choate was a blend of the skilled lawyer, the international diplomat, and the admired public figure. Although he never held political office, he was involved in politics all his life. From

Joseph Choate

1856 when he made a speech supporting John C. Frémont for president, to 1916 when he spoke in favor of Charles Evans Hughes, Choate was actively involved in every political issue of the day. His opinion was held in high esteem not only by his fellow lawyers but by the public as well.

Choate held many important positions. He was President of New York's 1894 Constitutional Convention. In 1899 he was appointed Ambassador to Great Britain and during his stay there, helped rebuild and buttress the friendship between the two nations. Choate was involved in settling the Alaskan boundary question, and worked closely with his friend Secretary of State Hay. He also was instrumental in the preliminary negotiations for the Panama Canal project. In 1907, Choate received his highest public honor when he was appointed Ambassador Extraordinary and led the American delegation to the Second Hague Conference, where he played a major role in the decisions made at the conference dealing with international law. Choate's arguments for an International Court and the sanctity of private property when on international waters were especially impressive.

In the last years of his life, Choate concentrated on bettering all aspects of the legal profession. For many years, he had been regarded as the "head of the bar" of New York City. He was a founder of the City Bar Association and its president in 1888 and 1889. He served as president of the New York State Bar Association in 1906 and 1908 and of the American Bar Association in 1898 and 1899. Choate was a lawyer who firmly believed in the greatness and integrity of his profession. The following passage shows the depth of his feelings:

I maintain that in no other occupation to which men can devote their lives is there a nobler intellectual pursuit or a higher moral standard than that which inspires and pervades the ranks of the legal profession. To establish justice, to maintain the rights of man, to defend the helpless and oppressed, to succor innocence, and to punish guilt, to aid in the solution of those great questions legal and constitutional which are constantly being evolved from the ever varying affairs and business of men are duties that may well challenge the best powers of man's intellect and the noblest qualities of the human heart.

When Choate died in May of 1917, Elihu Root said, "He has given his life for his country." To that must be added, "and for the ideals of his profession."

BENJAMIN CARDOZO was one of New York's finest lawyers and one of the country's greatest Supreme Court Justices. Nominated by Herbert Hoover in 1932 to replace the retiring Oliver Wendell Holmes, Cardozo soon earned the older justice's admiration:

I am sure that I should really love Cardozo if I knew him better. I not only owe to him some praise that I regard as one of the chief rewards of my life, but I have noticed such a sensitive delicacy in him that I tremble lest I should prove unworthy of his regard. All who know him seem to give him a superlative place. I have seen him but once, and then his face greatly impressed me. I believe he is a great and beautiful spirit.

Cardozo was born in New York City in 1870. His ancestors were Sephardic Jews. His great-great-grandfather, Aaron Nunez Cardozo, was a British merchant who emigrated to the colo-

Benjamin Cardozo

nies in the mid-1700's. His great-great-uncle, Rabbi Gershom Mendes Seixas, played a minor role in George Washington's inauguration. Cardozo's father, Albert, was a New York judge, who was forced to resign during the Boss Tweed scandals of the 1870's.

Young Cardozo's career bore no resemblance to his father's. He was a political science major at Columbia and graduated from Columbia Law School. Cardozo was admitted to the New York Bar in 1891. His years as a judge began in 1913, when he was elected justice of the supreme court in New York City. One month later, Governor William Sulzer appointed Cardozo to the Court of Appeals. The justices of that court had unanimously recommended him for the job. Cardozo was already well acquainted with the court's work, having published a study, *The Jurisdiction of the Court of Appeals of the State of New York,* in 1903.

Benjamin Cardozo was called a philosopher-judge, a man whose written opinions took on a distinctive, thoughtful, literary tone. This can be observed in his analysis of the purpose of the Court of Appeals:

The court exists not for the individual litigant but for the indefinite body of litigants, whose causes are potentially involved in the specific case at issue. The wrongs of the aggrieved suitors are only the algebraic symbols from which the court is to work out the formula of justice.

In 1927 Cardozo became chief judge of the court, a position he held in such precious regard that he turned down an appointment to the Permanent Court of International Arbitration at The Hague.

But a man of Cardozo's ability was destined for even greater things. In 1932 Herbert Hoover nominated him to the United States Supreme Court. He took the oath of office on March 14 of that year. On the Court he allied himself with the liberal elements and continued to show his literary prowess and his feeling for humanity. Legal historian Roscoe Pound wrote:

. . .his is an all round scholarship, and his culture, his wide general knowledge, and his command of English put him with the best of those who have sought to formulate judicial experience for the use of lawyers and litigants to come.

Cardozo was a pleasant, friendly man, with a great sensitivity to people and their needs. That sensitivity was obvious in his decisions, especially in that of *Helvering, Commissioner of Internal Revenue, et al., v. Davis,* a case which challenged the Social Security Act. Davis was a shareholder in the Edison Electric Company of Boston and wanted to stop his company from making the required social security payments. In upholding the law's constitutionality, Cardozo wrote the Court's majority opinion.

But the ill is all one, or at least not greatly different, whether men are thrown out of work because there is no longer work to do or because the disabilities of age make them incapable of doing it. Rescue becomes necessary irrespective of the cause. The hope behind this statute is to save men and women from the rigors of the poor house as well as from the haunting fear that such a lot awaits them when journey's end is near.
. . . More and more of our population is becoming urban and industrial instead of rural and agricultural. The evidence is impressive that among industrial workers the younger men and women are preferred over the older. In times of retrenchment the older are commonly the first to go, and even if retained,

their wages are likely to be lowered. The plight of the men and women at so low an age as forty is hard, almost hopeless, when they are driven to seek for reemployment.

These are not the words of a materialist. They are the words of a man who knew how to blend justice with compassion.

Beryl Levy, in his biography of Cardozo, published after the justice's death in 1938, wondered about the influence of his work. Comparing Cardozo's humanistic and philosophic approach to law with Holmes', Levy suggested that if that particular approach became popular, "Law practice will become less of a trade and more of a learned profession."

There can be no better eulogy to Benjamin Cardozo and his work.